THE 12 MOST INFLUENTIAL
PHOTOGRAPHS OF ALL TIME

by Marne Ventura

12 STORY LIBRARY

www.12StoryLibrary.com

12-Story Library is an imprint of Bookstaves and Press Room Editions

Produced for 12-Story Library by Red Line Editorial

Photographs ©: Dorothea Lange/Farm Security Administration/Office of War Information Black-and-White Negatives/Library of Congress, cover, 1, 11; Science & Society Picture Library/SSPL/Getty Images, 4; Frances Benjamin Johnston/Frances Benjamin Johnston Collection/Library of Congress, 5; Science Source, 6; clu/iStockphoto, 7; AP Images, 8, 13, 20, 26, 29; Farm Security Administration/Office of War Information Black-and-White Negatives/Library of Congress, 10; Alfred Eisenstaedt/The LIFE Picture Collection/Getty Images, 12; Will Counts Collection/Indiana University Archives, 14; JSC/NASA, 16, 28; MSFC/NASA, 17, 18; KSC/NASA, 19; David Hume Kennerly/Courtesy Gerald R. Ford Library, 21; Lacy Atkins/The San Francisco Examiner/AP Images, 23; 2001 The Record (Bergen Co. NJ)/Getty Images News/Getty Images, 24; Joe Rosenthal/AP Images, 25; Louie Favorite/The Journal & Constitution/AP Images, 27

Library of Congress Cataloging-in-Publication Data
Names: Ventura, Marne, author.
Title: The 12 most influential photographs of all time / by Marne Ventura.
Other titles: Twelve most influential photographs of all time
Description: Mankato, MN : 12 Story Library, 2017. | Series: The most
  influential | Includes bibliographical references and index. | Audience:
  Grades 4 to 6.
Identifiers: LCCN 2016047345 (print) | LCCN 2016048639 (ebook) | ISBN
  9781632354129 (hardcover : alk. paper) | ISBN 9781632354839 (pbk. : alk.
  paper) | ISBN 9781621435358 (hosted e-book)
Subjects: LCSH: Photography--Juvenile literature.
Classification: LCC TR149 .V46 2017 (print) | LCC TR149 (ebook) | DDC
  770--dc23
LC record available at https://lccn.loc.gov/2016047345

Printed in the United States of America
022017

Access free, up-to-date content on this topic plus a full digital version of this book. Scan the QR code on page 31 or use your school's login at 12StoryLibrary.com.

Table of Contents

Eadweard Muybridge Stops Motion

Eadweard Muybridge was an English photographer. As an adult, he moved to California. There, he began to experiment with photography of objects in motion. The human eye cannot see the separate movements of a moving object. But a camera can capture motion in split-second intervals.

In 1878, Muybridge took a series of photographs of a horse on a racetrack. To study the horse's gallop, Muybridge set up a row of cameras. A trip wire ran across the path of the horse. As the horse ran, it hit each wire. This caused the camera to snap the photos at split-second intervals.

Twelve of the sixteen images that are part of *Horse in Motion*

6

Number of years it took Muybridge to figure out how to show a horse's movement with photographs.

- Eadweard Muybridge experimented with motion photography in the 1870s.
- In his most famous experiment, Muybridge took a series of photographs of a horse running.
- The methods Muybridge created led to motion pictures.

ZOOPRAXISCOPE

Muybridge invented a brass and wood device called a zoopraxiscope. In Greek the word means "animal action viewer." Muybridge projected single images, such as the galloping horse, through the device. They appeared to move. It was the first movie projector.

The result of Muybridge's experiments at the racetrack is *Horse in Motion*. It is a set of 16 pictures. Each shot shows the position of the horse's legs as it moves. In the top middle photos, all the horse's hooves are off the ground.

Horse in Motion changed how people thought about photography. It led to the idea of creating sequences using still pictures. When shown quickly, frame by frame, the photos cause the human eye to see motion. This technique led to the invention of motion pictures.

Eadweard Muybridge

Wilhelm Roentgen's X-ray Transforms Medicine

Wilhelm Roentgen was a German physicist. In 1895, he was in his lab studying electron beams. In his experiments, he passed electron beams through a glass vacuum tube. He accidentally discovered that X-rays pass through flesh, but not bones or lead. Roentgen called the beams X-rays, since *x* stands for *unknown* in math.

Roentgen discovered that he could photograph an image made with X-rays. To show his discovery to other scientists, Roentgen made an X-ray image of his wife's left hand. It showed her bones and wedding ring.

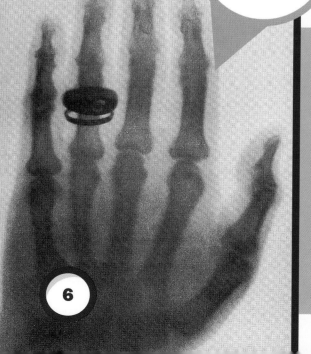

Wilhelm Roentgen's first X-ray

RADIATION

At the time of Roentgen's discovery, scientists thought X-rays were harmless. But researchers began to report burns and skin damage. Today, scientists know that exposure to high levels of X-rays can cause cancer. Low-level X-rays used to check for broken bones and cavities are generally considered safe.

90
Minutes required to take an X-ray in the 1890s, compared to 20 milliseconds today.

- During an experiment, Wilhelm Roentgen accidentally discovered X-rays.
- X-rays were a breakthrough in medical technology.
- Today, X-rays are used in many different fields.

THINK ABOUT IT

What other scientific breakthroughs can be both helpful and harmful?

The ability to see inside the human body transformed medicine. Before this time, the only way to see inside a patient's body was to make an incision. In March 1896, a hospital in Glasgow, Scotland, opened the world's first radiology department.

Technicians took X-rays of kidney stones, a penny lodged in a child's throat, and bullets inside a soldier's body.

Today, X-rays are still important in medicine. But they have become useful in other fields, too. At airports, security officers use X-ray scanners to check people and luggage for dangerous items. Astronomers use X-rays to study black holes and stars. Historians use them to read old documents that are too fragile to touch.

Airport X-ray scanners produce orange, blue, and green images based on what an item is made from.

Robert Wilson's Loch Ness Monster Inspires Skepticism

For 1,500 years, people have debated the legend of the Loch Ness Monster. Loch Ness is a large lake in Scotland. In 1933, a road was put in along the lake. Shortly afterward, a couple driving by the lake reported seeing an enormous animal. When the local paper wrote up the story, they called the animal a monster.

Word of the sighting brought more tourists to the area. An English newspaper hired Marmaduke Wetherell, a famous hunter,

Robert Wilson cropped his image to remove background details that would make the monster look small.

10

Approximate length, in inches (25 cm), of the toy monster's neck in Robert Wilson's photo.

- Robert Wilson took a photograph of the Loch Ness Monster in 1934.
- In 1994, one of the people involved with the photograph confessed it was a hoax.
- Today, the story of the photograph reminds readers to be skeptical.

to investigate. He found footprints of a 20-foot-long (6 m) animal. But when scientists analyzed the prints, they discovered a hoax. Someone had used a stuffed hippo foot to make the footprints.

The most convincing proof of the Loch Ness Monster came in 1934. That year, Robert Wilson took a grainy, black-and-white photograph that showed a creature's head rising from the water. He said he had been driving along Loch Ness, saw something moving in the lake, and took the photograph. People believed Wilson because he was a well-respected surgeon.

In 1994, Wetherell's stepson revealed new information about Wilson's photograph. The stepson confessed that Wetherell had been

angry and embarrassed that the footprints he found turned out to be fake. Wetherell, his stepson, and Wilson had created the photo for revenge. The monster was actually a toy sea serpent attached to a toy submarine.

For 60 years, many people had believed that the surgeon's photo proved the existence of the Loch Ness Monster. When it turned out to be a hoax, it showed the need for skepticism. It raised awareness that newspaper reports can be false, and that photographs can be altered.

Dorothea Lange Documents the Depression

From 1929 to 1939, the United States experienced the Great Depression. During this time, between 13 and 15 million Americans lost their jobs. The situation worsened when floods and dust storms destroyed farmlands during these years. Many farmers had to leave their land. They traveled west to find work.

During the Great Depression, President Franklin D. Roosevelt created the Resettlement Administration. One of its duties was to document the lives of migrant farmers. Dorothea Lange was a photographer who worked for the agency. Her job was to take pictures to show the need for federal aid and new laws.

Dorothea Lange

6

Number of shots Dorothea Lange took of the migrant mother and her children.

- Many Americans were out of work and homeless in the 1930s.
- The US government hired Dorothea Lange to photograph the poor.
- *Migrant Mother* represented the plight of migrant workers.

Migrant Mother

In March 1936, Lange happened upon a migrant worker camp in Nipomo, California. She took a photograph of a woman who sat in a makeshift tent with a baby asleep in her arms. Two children leaned against the woman, hiding their faces from the camera. The image showed the pain, suffering, and sadness of a migrant's life.

Lange's photograph, titled *Migrant Mother*, was printed in newspapers and magazines across the country. People were touched by the sadness of the photograph. It became an example of the ideal documentary photograph. It also became a symbol of the Great Depression.

Alfred Eisenstaedt Shoots a Victory Kiss

On December 7, 1941, Japan bombed Pearl Harbor, Hawaii. This attack spurred the United States to join World War II. For the next four years, battles raged in Europe and Asia. When Japan surrendered on August 14, 1945, the day was called Victory over Japan Day, or VJ-Day for short.

The nurse and sailor did not know each other.

People broke into spontaneous celebrations upon learning of World War II's end.

When Japan surrendered, Americans were elated. It meant World War II was over. Soldiers could stop fighting and come home to their families. In New York City's Times Square, people in restaurants, shops, and on the street cheered, kissed, and hugged.

Photographer Alfred Eisenstaedt was at Times Square during the celebration. He grabbed his camera and started taking pictures. One of them was a shot of a sailor kissing a nurse. Two weeks later, Eisenstaedt's photograph appeared on the cover of *Life* magazine. It reflected the joy people felt at the war's end.

PHOTOJOURNALISM

Traditional journalists tell news stories through writing. Eisenstaedt was a different kind of journalist. He told news stories through photographs. This type of reporting is called photojournalism.

405,399
Number of American deaths in WWII.

- Japan surrendered on August 14, 1945, bringing World War II to an end.
- After five years of war, people celebrated when they heard the news.
- Eisenstaedt's photo became a symbol of the war's end.

Will Counts Raises Awareness for Civil Rights

In the 1950s, the civil rights movement was gaining strength in the United States. The goal of this movement was to gain equal treatment for black people. While this was required by law, it often did not happen. This was especially true in the South.

Many schools in many Southern states were segregated. White children went to one school, while black children went to another. Schools for white children received more funds, better-trained teachers, and nicer buildings.

Will Counts captured Hazel Bryan's raw anger and Elizabeth Eckford's calm determination.

Will Counts Collection:
Indiana University Archives

15

Elizabeth Eckford's age in the photograph.

- A US Supreme Court decision outlawed segregation in schools.
- The governor of Arkansas used soldiers to block nine black students from entering Little Rock Central High School.
- Will Counts's photograph raised awareness of the struggle for civil rights.

THINK ABOUT IT

What information can a photograph give to people that a written article cannot? How does this make an image a powerful tool for reporters?

In 1954, the US Supreme Court ruled that segregated public schools were illegal. Some schools refused to change. This situation led to violence when black students tried to attend white schools.

In 1957, nine black students enrolled in Little Rock Central High School in Arkansas. The state's governor, and many white citizens, opposed black students going to school there. The governor ordered the National Guard to block the school's doors. A white mob also gathered in front of the school. The mob threw rocks at the students and threatened them.

Reporter Will Counts took photos of the event. The most famous photo shows a black student, Elizabeth Eckford, walking toward the high school. A white student scowls at her back. Counts's photograph recorded an important moment in civil rights history. It drew attention to the fight for equal civil rights.

36 SHOTS

At the time that Counts took the picture, most photographers used cameras with film that had to be reloaded after each shot. Counts used a new kind of camera that let him snap 36 photos before reloading. This increased his chance of getting the best shot of an event.

William Anders Shares a New View of Earth

During the 1960s, the United States and the Soviet Union had competing space programs. A strong space program was a sign of a powerful country. At first, the Soviet Union was in the lead. In 1957, it launched Sputnik, the world's first satellite. A little more than three years later, the Soviet Union sent the first human into space.

The United States launched its own manned spacecraft in 1968. It was called Apollo 8. Its mission was to be the first round-trip human visit to the moon.

William Anders's photo gave people a new perspective of Earth.

It was the first time any person would see the dark side of the moon. Astronauts Frank Borman, James Lovell Jr., and William Anders entered moon's orbit on December 24, 1968.

While circling the moon for the fourth time, Anders noticed the earth rising above the horizon. The men grabbed cameras and began snapping photographs. Anders captured a color image of Earth. Its lower half was in darkness, hanging above the rocky surface of the moon.

Anders's photograph is one of the most reproduced space photographs

800

Estimated number of photographs the astronauts of Apollo 8 took on their mission.

- Apollo 8 was the first human flight to the moon.
- During the fourth orbit of the moon, Anders noticed the Earth over the horizon.
- *Earthrise* helped inspire the environmental movement.

of all time. For many people, seeing the greens and blues of Earth's plants and water made them realize how precious the planet's resources are. For this reason, *Earthrise* is credited for inspiring the environmental movement. Its followers fought to protect Earth. They demanded clean water and air to save the planet.

NASA crews launched Apollo 8 on December 21, 1968.

SURPRISE!

Anders said that seeing Earth during the moon mission was a surprise. He explains, "We were focused on the moon, observing the moon, studying the moon, and the Earth was not really in our thoughts until it popped up above that horizon."

17

Buzz Aldrin Jr. Photographs His Footprint

In 1961, President John F. Kennedy promised that the nation would land an American on the moon before the end of the decade. It seemed impossible. But scientists at NASA worked hard to achieve it.

Aldrin photographed his footprint as part of a study on the moon's surface.

21.5

Hours Neil Armstrong and Edwin "Buzz" Aldrin Jr. spent on the moon's surface.

- Apollo 11 landed on the moon in 1969.
- Armstrong was the first human to set foot on the moon.
- Aldrin's photo symbolizes the accomplishment.

The Apollo 11 crew, from left to right: Neil Armstrong, Michael Collins, and Edwin Aldrin Jr.

In July 1969, NASA launched Apollo 11. Its crew was Michael Collins, Neil Armstrong, and Edwin "Buzz" Aldrin Jr. On July 20, Collins orbited while Armstrong and Aldrin became the first humans to land on the moon. During their moonwalk, Aldrin took a photo of his footprint in the moon's powdery surface.

The spacewalk changed how people learned of scientific news.

In the past, people had learned about scientific breakthroughs after they happened. Apollo 11's moon landing was the first time people around the world watched this type of event in real time on television.

Historians believe the moon landing was one of the most important events of the 20th century. The photograph of a human footprint on the moon represented the advances humans had made in science. It also showed how something that seemed impossible could be done.

Photographers Record the Vietnam War's End

In the 1950s, North and South Vietnam began to disagree. North Vietnam wanted Vietnam to be one country with a communist government. South Vietnam wanted democracy. The US government wanted to support democracy.

In 1965, US soldiers began to help the South Vietnamese. By 1969, more than 500,000 US troops were stationed in Vietnam. Meanwhile, China and the Soviet Union aided North Vietnam.

Many Americans did not support the decision to send soldiers to Vietnam. Some people protested the war.

Communist forces overtook the city of Saigon in April 1975.

They became less trusting of the government. Others felt the government had meant to do the right thing but that it could not succeed in winning the war.

By 1973, the US government decided to begin withdrawing its troops from Vietnam. It could no longer bear the cost in money and in lives. In 1975, South Vietnam's president surrendered. An Associated Press photographer took a shot of a North Vietnamese tank. It was rolling through the gates of the president's palace in the city of Saigon.

The photograph reflected defeat for Americans. Ten years of fighting had not prevented the communists from overtaking South Vietnam. Thousands of people had died in the war. It had also sharply divided US society. Those who supported the war and those who did not clashed often.

60,000

Approximate number of Americans who died in the Vietnam War.

- North and South Vietnam began fighting in the 1950s.
- The United States began sending troops to Vietnam in 1965 to fight communism.
- In 1973, US troops pulled out of the war, and South Vietnam surrendered in 1975.

President Gerald Ford announced the end of US involvement in Vietnam on April 23, 1975.

Robert Beck Captures a Soccer Triumph

The US soccer team played China in the Women's World Cup in California on July 10, 1999. During 120 minutes of tough battle, neither team scored. After two overtimes and nine penalty kicks, Brandi Chastain was next to take the US team's penalty kick.

Four months earlier, Chastain had lost a game by missing a penalty kick to the same goalkeeper. Since that time, she had worked on using her left foot instead of her right. Her coach put her in, hoping to confuse the goalkeeper.

Chastain was nervous. The outcome of the game was riding on her kick. The sold-out stadium was silent. Forty million fans were watching the game on television. Chastain was hot and exhausted. She loved soccer and had worked hard for years to be part of this team.

Chastain tried to relax. She focused on the kick. When the ball flew past the goalkeeper to win the game, Chastain was overcome with joy. She ripped off her soccer jersey and swung it in the air. She dropped to her knees, cheering. Photographer Robert Beck snapped a photo of Chastain at that moment.

90,125
Number of fans at the Rose Bowl watching the game-winning kick.

- Chastain scored on an overtime penalty kick during the Women's World Cup in 1999.
- The photo captured her joy and excitement.
- It raised enthusiasm for women's sports.

The emotion Robert Beck captured in Brandi Chastain became a symbol of triumph.

Newsweek, *Time*, and *Sports Illustrated* put the photo on their covers. The photo of Chastain also became a symbol of the new popularity of women's soccer.

At the time of the photo, there were 75 women's college soccer teams in the United States. Today, that number has risen to more than 300.

Thomas E. Franklin Photographs Patriotism

A terrorist group called al-Qaeda declared a holy war on the United States. As part of the war, Islamic extremists hijacked four American planes on September 11, 2001. Two of the planes were flown from Boston, Massachusetts, toward the Twin Towers of the World Trade Center in New York City.

The hijacked planes crashed into the Twin Towers. Both towers exploded and collapsed. Firefighters, police officers, and other emergency workers rushed to the scene. They worked tirelessly throughout the day. Nearly 3,000 people died, and 10,000 people were injured.

Thomas E. Franklin was a photographer for a New Jersey newspaper.

The firefighters' display of patriotism touched many Americans after the 9/11 attacks.

RAISING FLAGS

Thomas E. Franklin's 9/11 image is often compared to one by Joe Rosenthal. In 1945, Rosenthal photographed six marines raising a US flag at Iwo Jima, Japan, during World War II. Both photos have similar colors and composition. Both images also highlight American heroes. They carry the same message of American strength and pride.

When news of the attack reached his office, he went to the site of the attack. Franklin took many photos of the incident. His shot of three firefighters raising an American flag quickly gained attention.

Franklin's photograph became a symbol of 9/11. The firefighters are covered in dust. Behind them, the former skyscrapers are a pile of rubble. The dominant gray of the photo is broken by the brilliant red, white, and blue of the flag. The image became a symbol of hope and patriotism amid tragedy.

Raising the flag on Iwo Jima

400
Number of firefighters and police officers who died in service on 9/11.

- Islamic extremists destroyed the World Trade Center on September 11, 2001.
- Firefighters, police officers, and other emergency personnel rushed to the towers to help.
- Franklin's photo became a symbol of patriotism.

25

Louie Favorite Shows a Mother's Love

For many years, women could not serve in the military. Before World War I, nurses and other women helped alongside men. But they did not get the same opportunities and benefits. Slowly the military began opening its doors to women. Today, women can serve in combat and in many other roles.

A 1948 law made women permanent, regular members of the US military.

One of the women who chose to serve was Terri Gurrola. She joined the army and trained as a physician's assistant. Then Gurrola served in Iraq.

When Gurrola left for Iraq, her daughter Gaby was two years old. Gurrola missed Gaby terribly while she was away. Her biggest fear was that Gaby would not remember her.

90
Percentage of military occupations open to women as of 2016.

- Women had limited roles in the US military in the past.
- Major Terri Gurrola was a physician's assistant who served in Iraq in 2007.
- The photo of Gurrola's reunion with her daughter became a symbol of women and families in the military.

On September 11, 2007, Gurrola flew into Atlanta, Georgia, after seven months overseas. As Gurrola got off the plane, she heard Gaby call out, "Mommy!"

Gurrola ran across the airport, slid onto her knees, and hugged her daughter. She didn't want to let go. She was crying hard because she was so happy. When Gurrola finally looked up, everyone in the airport was crying, too.

News photographer Louie Favorite captured an image of the emotional moment.

The image of Gurrola was widely printed in newspapers, in magazines, and on posters. It became a symbol for awareness of women in the military. It reminded people about the sacrifices and hardships service members endure to serve their country.

Terri Gurrola and her daughter depicted a modern image of female soldiers.

Other Notable Photographs

Anne Frank

Six million Jews were killed during WWII. Anne Frank was a teenage girl who kept a diary of her experience as she hid with her family in an attic in Amsterdam. *The Diary of Anne Frank* became a classic story of a young girl's view of the Holocaust. Her portrait captures her innocence and youth. It became a symbol of the tragedy of young lives lost.

John F. Kennedy Jr.'s Salute

On November 22, 1963, an assassin killed US President John F. Kennedy. The world was shocked and saddened. Photographer Dan Farrell was assigned to cover the funeral. He photographed the president's son, John Jr. Though he was only three, John Jr. stood saluting his father. The image reminded Americans to be brave amid a tragedy.

Barack Obama Wins the Election

In 2008, Barack Obama won the presidential election and became the first black US president. The photograph shows Obama and his family walking amid supporters on election night 2008. The photograph records the excitement many Americans felt to see the nation's first black president.

US Airways on Hudson River

On January 15, 2009, during a routine flight from New York to North Carolina, a flock of birds flew right into the plane's engines. Both engines shut down, and the plane began to fall. The pilot and copilot landed the plane safely on the Hudson River. A photographer captured an image of the passengers exiting the plane along its wing. The photograph showed the power of keeping calm in stressful situations.

Glossary

composition
The way smaller parts are arranged to form a whole image.

documentary
A movie, television program, or series of photographs that tells a story based on facts and evidence.

electron beam
A stream of negative particles called electrons.

hijack
To use force to make a pilot or driver go to a specific place.

hoax
An act meant as a trick.

incision
The cut a doctor makes during surgery.

interval
An amount of time between separate events.

migrant
A person who moves from place to place in search of work.

radiology
A branch of science that uses X-rays.

segregation
Separating people by race.

skepticism
An attitude of doubt.

trip wire
A wire set close to the ground that, when moved, causes a reaction.

vacuum tube
A scientific tool that allows electricity to pass freely.

For More Information

Books

Honovich, Nancy. *Guide to Photography*. National Geographic: Washington, DC, 2015.

Nardo, Don. *The Blue Marble: How a Photograph Revealed Earth's Fragile Beauty*. Compass Point Books: Mankato, MN, 2014.

Tougas, Shelley. *Little Rock Girl 1957: How a Photograph Changed the Fight for Integration*. Compass Point Books: Mankato, MN, 2012.

Visit 12StoryLibrary.com

Scan the code or use your school's login at **12StoryLibrary.com** for recent updates about this topic and a full digital version of this book. Enjoy free access to:

- Digital ebook
- Breaking news updates
- Live content feeds
- Videos, interactive maps, and graphics
- Additional web resources

Note to educators: Visit 12StoryLibrary.com/register to sign up for free premium website access. Enjoy live content plus a full digital version of every 12-Story Library book you own for every student at your school.

Editor's note: The 12 topics featured in this book are selected by the author and approved by the book's editor. While not a definitive list, the selected topics are an attempt to balance the book's subject with the intended readership. To expand learning about this subject, please visit **12StoryLibrary.com** or use this book's QR code to access free additional content.

Index

About the Author

Marne Ventura is the author of 45 books for children, both nonfiction and fiction. She loves writing about history, science, technology, arts and crafts, health, and food. Ventura and her husband live on the central coast of California, near the spot where *Migrant Mother* was taken.